# MAHABHARATA

THE BLIND KING DHRITARASHTRA OF HASTINAPURA HAD A HUNDRED SONS— DURYODHANA, DUHSHASANA AND OTHERS, WHO WERE TOGETHER CALLED THE KAURAVAS. THEIR FIVE COUSINS— YUDHISHTHIRA, THE TRUTHFUL, BHEEMA THE STRONG-ARMED, ARJUNA, THE MAN OF SKILL, NAKULA AND SAHADEVA WERE THE PANDAVAS. FROM THEIR BOYHOOD, THE KAURAVAS HATED THE PANDAVAS, FEARING THAT THEY MIGHT INHERIT THE KINGDOM.

THEY POISONED BHEEMA'S FOOD AND THREW HIM INTO A RIVER.

WHERE AM I?

THEY TRIED TO BURN THE PANDAVAS IN A HOUSE MADE OF LAC.

WE WILL BE SAFE IN THE JUNGLES.

THE PANDAVAS ESCAPED ALL THESE WICKED PLANS TO DESTROY THEM. THEIR MARRIAGE TO DRAUPADI, DAUGHTER OF KING DRUPADA, MADE THEM POWERFUL.

FINALLY, WISDOM PREVAILED ON KING DHRITARASHTRA AFTER LISTENING TO THE ADVICE OF SUCH LEARNED MEN AS...

BHEESHMA, THE OLDEST MEMBER OF THE ROYAL FAMILY.

VIDURA, THE WISEST MAN IN THE COURT.

DRONA, THE MILITARY EXPERT AND TEACHER OF THE PRINCES.

HE GAVE HALF THE KINGDOM TO THE PANDAVAS, WHO BUILT A GREAT CITY, INDRAPRASTHA, AND RULED WISELY.

THE RAJASUYA YAGNA HAS MADE YOU KING OF KINGS, YUDHISHTHIRA.

THANKS TO YOUR GUIDANCE, LORD KRISHNA!

THE SUCCESS OF THE PANDAVAS MADE DURYODHANA VERY JEALOUS.

WE MUST FIGHT THEM, DUHSHASANA

WE CAN'T FIGHT THEM. CAN WE, UNCLE SHAKUNI?

WHY DON'T YOU INVITE YUDHISHTHIRA TO A GAME OF DICE?

DURYODHANA WAS PLEASED WHEN YUDHISHTHIRA ACCEPTED HIS INVITATION.

WELCOME, BROTHER! UNCLE SHAKUNI WILL PLAY WITH YOU ON MY BEHALF

SHAKUNI! HE IS THE DEVIL HIMSELF! BUT IF I REFUSE TO PLAY, IT MAY CREATE ILLWILL.

THE GAME BEGAN IN THE PRESENCE OF THE KING AND HIS WELL-WISHERS.

YOU WILL HAVE TO STAKE SOMETHING.

I STAKE MY JEWELS.

YUDHISHTHIRA CAST THE DICE.

I STAKE MY HORSES, MY CHARIOTS, MY ELEPHANTS.

LOST... LOST... LOST...

YUDHISHTHIRA WAS BLINDLY CARRIED AWAY BY THE GAME.

I'VE LOST MY ENTIRE KINGDOM! I NOW STAKE MY BROTHER, NAKULA.

LOST!

ARJUNA! OUR ELDER BROTHER HAS LOST HIS SENSES.

OH GOD! I HAVE LOST ALL MY BROTHERS. I STAKE MYSELF.

LOST AGAIN!

I HAVE LOST EVERYTHING.

NO... NOT EVERYTHING. YOU STILL POSSESS WHAT IS DEAREST TO YOU - DRAUPADI!

THE GAME TOOK SO BAD A TURN THAT THOSE WHO LOOKED ON WERE SHOCKED.

WELL, I STAKE DRAUPADI!

HE HAD NO RIGHT TO STAKE HER.

LOST HER TOO!

YES SHE IS THE WIFE OF THE FIVE PANDAVAS.

DURYODHANA ROSE, FLUSHED WITH VICTORY.

BROTHER DUHSHASANA! GO AND BRING DRAUPADI HERE.

SOON—

HERE IS OUR SLAVE GIRL.

HELP! HELP!

BHEEMA COULD NOT CONTAIN HIS ANGER.

OUR BROTHER'S HANDS HAVE BROUGHT RUIN TO US! SAHADEVA, BRING SOME FIRE - I WILL BURN THEM.

NO! NO! BHEEMA! CONTROL YOUR ANGER!

DUHSHASANA FURTHER INSULTED DRAUPADI BY PULLING OFF HER SARI.

FIVE HUSBANDS AND NOT ONE WILL SAVE ME!

I'D RATHER BE BLIND THAN SEE THIS.

THEN, BY THE GRACE OF LORD KRISHNA, A MIRACLE TOOK PLACE.

SARI WITHIN SARI

A MIRACLE!

GOD HAS SAVED HER!

THE SHAMEFUL ACT OF HIS SONS MADE DHRITARASHTRA SAD.

MY SON HAS WON YOUR KINGDOM BY TRICKERY. I RETURN IT TO YOU. GO AND LIVE IN PEACE.

ONCE AGAIN DURYODHANA CHALLENGED YUDHISHTHIRA TO A GAME OF DICE AND YUDHISHTHIRA PLAYED WITH RENEWED HOPE.

LIVE THERE FOR TWELVE YEARS. THEN FOR ONE MORE YEAR YOU WILL HIDE YOURSELVES FROM THE WORLD. IF YOU ARE FOUND OUT, ANOTHER TWELVE YEARS IN THE JUNGLE FOR YOU.'

YOU MUST WAGER THAT IF YOU LOSE, YOU AND YOUR FAMILY WILL RETIRE TO THE FOREST.

AGAIN YUDHISHTHIRA LOST. AFTER BOWING TO BHEESHMA AND THE OTHER ELDERS THE PANDAVAS LEFT THE CITY. KUNTI, THEIR MOTHER, AND THEIR CHILDREN STAYED BEHIND.

BLESS ME THAT I MAY HAVE STRENGTH TO ENDURE THE DIFFICULT DAYS AHEAD.

A CURSE BE ON THOSE KAURAVAS!

FOR YEARS, THE PANDAVAS WANDERED IN THE FORESTS. THEY HAD ADVENTURES WITH WILD BEASTS, DEMONS AND SAVAGES.

PUT THOSE SPEARS DOWN OR ELSE...

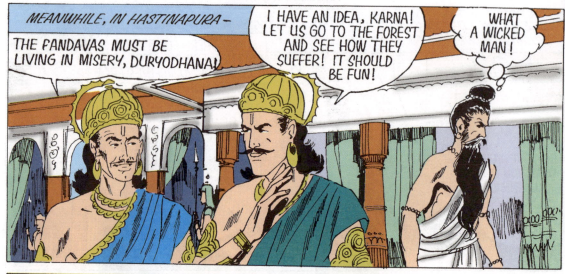

MEANWHILE, IN HASTINAPURA—

THE PANDAVAS MUST BE LIVING IN MISERY, DURYODHANA!

I HAVE AN IDEA, KARNA! LET US GO TO THE FOREST AND SEE HOW THEY SUFFER! IT SHOULD BE FUN!

WHAT A WICKED MAN!

DURYODHANA AND HIS FRIEND KARNA WENT TO THE FOREST WITH A LARGE ARMY. WHEN THEY WERE ABOUT TO SET UP A CAMP—

NO! YOU CAN'T PUT UP YOUR TENTS HERE!

THE FOREST DWELLERS, THE GANDHARVAS, WERE VICTORIOUS IN THE BATTLE THAT FOLLOWED.

THIS WILL TEACH HIM A LESSON.

NOW YOU ARE OUR PRISONER!

THE NEWS REACHED THE PANDAVAS.

THAT'S WONDERFUL! HA! HA! HA!

NO, BHEEMA! YOU SHOULDN'T LAUGH AT YOUR COUSIN WHEN HE IS IN DISTRESS. GO AND RESCUE HIM.

THE GANDHARVA CHIEF WAS DEFEATED BY ARJUNA.

ARJUNA, I WILL DO AS YOU WISH!

DURYODHANA WAS FREED.

I AM AN UNHAPPY MAN, KARNA! I FEEL HUMILIATED. AND EVEN IN THE FOREST THEY SEEM HAPPY.

DID YOU SEE HIS FACE, ARJUNA?

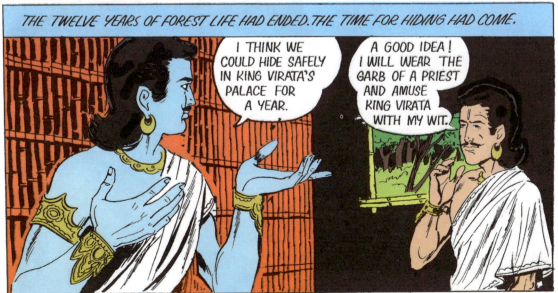

THE TWELVE YEARS OF FOREST LIFE HAD ENDED. THE TIME FOR HIDING HAD COME.

I THINK WE COULD HIDE SAFELY IN KING VIRATA'S PALACE FOR A YEAR.

A GOOD IDEA! I WILL WEAR THE GARB OF A PRIEST AND AMUSE KING VIRATA WITH MY WIT.

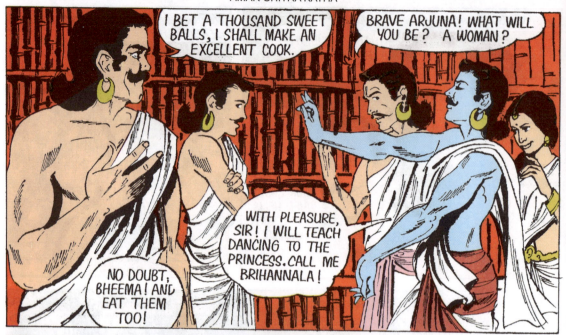

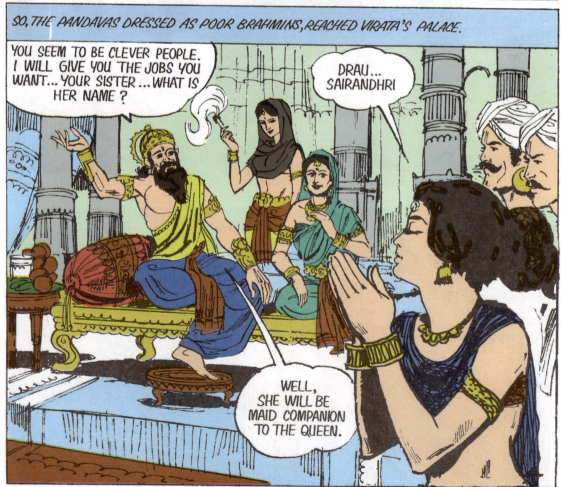

SUDDENLY A FIGURE JUMPED ON HIM.

I HAVE BEEN CHEATED.

YOU DESERVED IT, YOU VILLAIN!

KEECHAKA WAS KILLED IN THE FIERCE DUEL.

THERE! I HAVE KEPT MY PROMISE TO DRAUPADI.

NEXT DAY—

THEY SAY KEECHAKA DIED IN AN ACCIDENT!

GOOD RIDDANCE! NOBODY LIKED HIM, NOT EVEN THE KING.

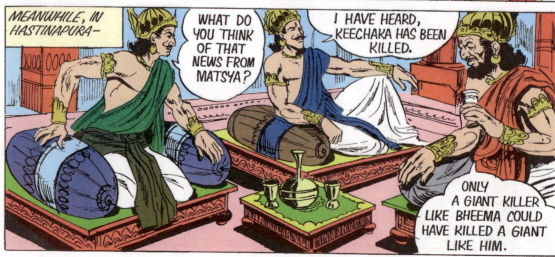

MEANWHILE, IN HASTINAPURA—

WHAT DO YOU THINK OF THAT NEWS FROM MATSYA?

I HAVE HEARD, KEECHAKA HAS BEEN KILLED.

ONLY A GIANT KILLER LIKE BHEEMA COULD HAVE KILLED A GIANT LIKE HIM.

LET'S ATTACK KING VIRATA FROM THE NORTH AND LET THE KING OF TRIGARTA ATTACK HIM FROM THE SOUTH.

GOOD! IF THE PANDAVAS ARE HIDING THERE, THEY ARE SURE TO HELP KING VIRATA AND WILL BE FOUND OUT.

IN THE COURT OF VIRATA —

THE KING OF TRIGARTA HAS ATTACKED US.

IF YOU PERMIT ME, SIR, MY BROTHER AND I CAN HELP YOU IN ROUTING THE ENEMY.

THE KING WAS ASTONISHED TO SEE THE SKILL OF HIS PRIEST AND COOK IN WIELDING THE BOW.

THE BATTLE WAS FIERCE AND THE ENEMY RECEIVED A CRUSHING DEFEAT.

MEANWHILE, THE NEWS WAS RECEIVED IN THE CAPITAL BY PRINCE UTTARA THAT THEY WERE BEING ATTACKED FROM THE NORTH BY THE KAURAVA ARMY.

NOBLE PRINCE! IN THE ABSENCE OF THE KING YOU HAVE TO FACE THE KAURAVA ARMY!

SURE! SURE! IF ONLY I HAD A CHARIOTEER, I COULD LEAD AN ARMY!

DRAUPADI, WHO HAD HEARD HIM BRAG, LAUGHED.

YOUR HIGHNESS! BRIHANNALA IS A DRIVER OF GREAT SKILL.

BRIHANNALA! A WOMAN! A DANCER!

SOON A CHARIOT DRIVEN BY "BRIHANNALA" ARRIVED NEAR THE PALACE.

THERE SHE IS! I CANNOT BACK OUT NOW!

KARNA, DRONA AND BHEESHMA FOUGHT HIM ONE BY ONE

I FEEL ASHAMED TO BE DEFEATED BY A WOMAN!

SHE IS NOT A WOMAN. IT IS ARJUNA, THE PRINCE AMONG ARCHERS.

UTTARA RETURNED VICTORIOUS FROM THE BATTLE-FIELD!

KING VIRATA HAD RETURNED BY THEN TO HIS CAPITAL.

BRAVO, UTTARA!

FATHER! IT IS ARJUNA WHO HAS WON THIS VICTORY FOR US. YOU KNOW HIM AS BRIHANNALA!

NOW, I SEE IT ALL. SO THIS PRIEST IS THE GREAT YUDHISHTHIRA. THE COOK IS BHEEMA! PARDON ME, PRINCES, IF I HAVE UNKNOWINGLY HURT YOU AT ANY TIME.

17

THE COURT OF HASTINAPURA~

GIVE THE PANDAVAS AT LEAST FIVE VILLAGES. OTHERWISE THERE MAY BE WAR!

LET IT BE WAR THEN! WE WON'T PART WITH AN INCH OF OUR SOIL.

YES, WAR! WAR!

KRISHNA HAD TO RETURN DISAPPOINTED TO THE MATSYA KINGDOM.

I HAVE FAILED IN MY BID FOR PEACE!

IT IS A DAY OF SORROW.

IF THEY WANT WAR, LET THEM HAVE IT.

JUST BEFORE THE WAR, DURYODHANA AND ARJUNA WENT TO SEEK KRISHNA'S HELP.

I LOVE YOU BOTH! ONE OF YOU MUST CHOOSE ME. THE OTHER WILL HAVE MY ARMY.

ARJUNA IS A FOOL! I'LL HAVE THE STRONG YADAVA ARMY ON MY SIDE.

I CHOOSE YOU, OH KRISHNA. BE ON OUR SIDE.

PREPARATIONS FOR WAR WERE COMPLETE. KRISHNA ACCEPTED THE HUMBLE ROLE OF ARJUNA'S CHARIOTEER.

BHEESHMA BECAME THE COMMANDER-IN-CHIEF OF THE KAURAVAS.

THE FIELD OF KURUKSHETRA PRESENTED AN AWESOME SPECTACLE. THE KAURAVAS HAD SPREAD IN A VAST SEMI CIRCLE TO MAKE THE FIRST MOVE. THE PANDAVAS HAD ARRANGED THEIR ARMIES IN A NEEDLE-LIKE FORMATION.

THE AIR WAS SHRILL WITH THE NOISE OF DRUMS, CONCHES, TRUMPETS AND THE CLANK, CLANK OF WEAPONS.

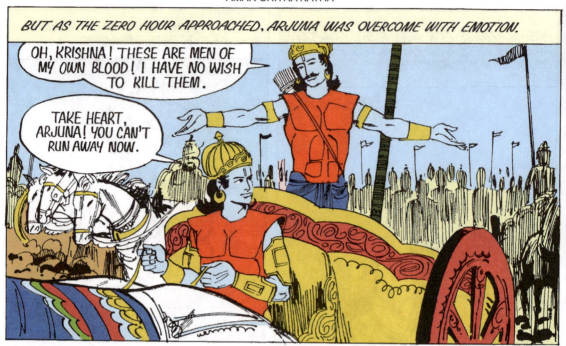

LOOK AT ARJUNA! HIS CHARIOT IS AS SWIFT AS HIS ARROWS.

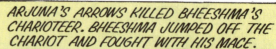

ARJUNA'S ARROWS KILLED BHEESHMA'S CHARIOTEER. BHEESHMA JUMPED OFF THE CHARIOT AND FOUGHT WITH HIS MACE.

JUST THEN THE SUN SET AND THE FIGHTING ALSO STOPPED.

ON THE FOURTH DAY—

BHEEMA IS CREATING HAVOC. ATTACK HIM WITH THE BATTALION OF ELEPHANTS.

UNBELIEVABLE! HAS ONE MAN DONE SO MUCH DAMAGE!

IT LOOKS AS THOUGH WE ARE IN A MOUNTAINOUS DISTRICT!

BHEEMA SCATTERED THE ELEPHANTS WITH HIS MIGHTY MACE.

WITH EACH SUCCEEDING DAY, THE WAR INCREASED IN FURY.

ON THE NINTH NIGHT IN PANDAVA CAMP...

OUR ONLY HOPE LIES IN GETTING RID OF BHEESHMA.

LET SHIKHANDI CONFRONT HIM IN THE BATTLE TOMORROW. GRANDFATHER MAY NOT FIGHT HIM BECAUSE HE WAS BORN A WOMAN. I HAVE AN IDEA.

ON THE TENTH DAY—

NO, I DON'T WANT TO FIGHT SHIKHANDI. BUT HOW IS IT THAT HIS ARROWS ARE SO WELL-AIMED! AH... THEY ARE ARJUNA'S ARROWS.

BHEESHMA FELL, HIS BODY PIERCED IN MANY PLACES BY THE ARROWS OF ARJUNA.

WHEN THE FIGHTING ENDED FOR THE DAY, FRIENDS AS WELL AS FOES GATHERED AROUND THE OLD MAN.

I HAVE A BED OF ARROWS, ARJUNA! MAKE ME A PILLOW. I NEED WATER TOO.

THREE ARROWS FROM ARJUNA'S BOW GAVE HIM A PILLOW AND ONE ARROW STRUCK DEEP INTO THE EARTH, GAVE WATER.

GOOD! I WILL NOW REST AND AWAIT MY DEATH ON MY APPOINTED DAY!

DRONA NOW BECAME THE COMMANDER-IN-CHIEF OF THE KAURAVA ARMY.

ACHARYA! LET'S CAPTURE YUDHISHTHIRA ALIVE.

YES, DURYODHANA

ARJUNA CAME TO YUDHISHTHIRA'S RESCUE.

I MUST GO BACK ARJUNA'S ARROWS ARE COMING TOO FAST.

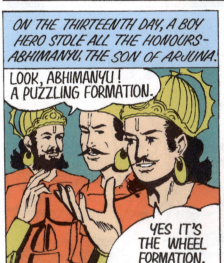

ON THE THIRTEENTH DAY, A BOY HERO STOLE ALL THE HONOURS- ABHIMANYU, THE SON OF ARJUNA.

LOOK, ABHIMANYU! A PUZZLING FORMATION.

YES IT'S THE WHEEL FORMATION.

ABHIMANYU PLUNGED HEROICALLY IN.

FOLLOW HIM, HE MAY BE TRAPPED.

BUT PRINCE YUDHISHTHIRA! WICKED JAYADRATHA HAS SEALED THE ENTRANCE.

ABHIMANYU FOUGHT BRAVELY.

KARNA! KILL HIS HORSES AND CHARIOTEER.

AN ARROW SHOT BY KARNA SMASHED ABHIMANYU'S BOW.

HE FOUGHT WITH A SWORD BUT DRONA'S ARROW BROKE IT

SOON ABHIMANYU LAY DEAD IN THE BATTLE-FIELD.

WHEN THE SAD NEWS REACHED ARJUNA, HE TOOK A TERRIBLE OATH.

BEFORE SUNSET TOMORROW, I SHALL KILL JAYADRATHA OR SWALLOW FIRE.

DRONA WAS DETERMINED TO SAVE JAYADRATHA.

LET JAYADRATHA BE IN THE CENTRE. LET WARRIORS PROTECT HIM ON ALL SIDES.

ARJUNA WAS EQUALLY DETERMINED TO KILL JAYADRATHA, BUT THE DAY WAS COMING TO A CLOSE.

THE SUN WILL SET IN AN HOUR AND JAYADRATHA IS STILL FAR AWAY, KRISHNA!

THEN ALL OF A SUDDEN—

IT IS ALREADY DARK! THE SUN HAS SET.

ARJUNA MUST SWALLOW FIRE NOW.

BUT THE SUN HAD REALLY NOT SET.

IT WAS A TRICK I PLAYED. BE PREPARED NOW.

ARJUNA'S CHARIOT RUSHED FORWARD.

AND SOON—

JAYADRATHA IS DEAD.

ABHIMANYU IS AVENGED!

ANOTHER TRICK ON THE FIFTEENTH DAY... WHEN DRONA PROVED UNCONQUERABLE. BHEEMA SHOUTED—

THAT'S THE END OF ASHWATTHAMA!

YUDHISHTHIRA, HAVE THEY KILLED MY SON?

YES, BHEEMA HAS KILLED... AN ELEPHANT NAMED ASHWATTHAMA.

DRONA COULD NOT BEAR THE SHOCK OF THE NEWS. HE WAS SOON KILLED BY THE SWORD OF A WARRIOR IN THE PANDAVA ARMY.

MY SON! MY SON!

KARNA NOW BECAME THE COMMANDER-IN-CHIEF. HE LED THE ATTACK SUPPORTED BY DUHSHASANA AND OTHERS. BHEEMA CHALLENGED DUHSHASANA.

DUHSHASANA! I HAVE A SCORE TO SETTLE WITH YOU.

IN THE COMBAT, DUHSHASANA FELL.

BEFORE KILLING YOU, I'LL TEAR OFF THE HAND THAT INSULTED DRAUPADI.

KARNA FOUGHT WITH ARJUNA, HIS SERPENT LIKE ARROWS CHASED ARJUNA WHEREVER HE WENT.

THEN ARJUNA HAD HIS OPPORTUNITY. KARNA'S CHARIOT WAS CAUGHT IN THE MUD.

A LITTLE PUSH AND THIS WILL COME OUT OF THE MUD.

ARJUNA'S ARROWS CONTINUED TO COME WHIZZING THROUGH THE AIR.

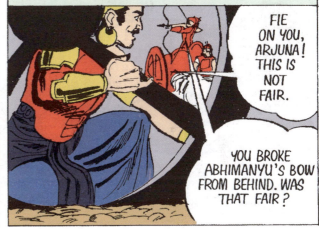

FIE ON YOU, ARJUNA! THIS IS NOT FAIR.

YOU BROKE ABHIMANYU'S BOW FROM BEHIND. WAS THAT FAIR?

AND THEN A CRESCENT-HEADED ARROW CAME WHIZZING FROM ARJUNA'S BOW.

THE GREAT KARNA BEHEADED.

DURYODHANA WAS SHOCKED AT THE NEWS.

MY DEAREST FRIEND, MY FONDEST HOPE GONE!

MORE SHOCKS FOLLOWED.

WHAT! SHALYA ALSO HAS FALLEN!

THE KAURAVA ARMY WAS SHATTERED:

SHAKUNI IS ALSO DEAD AND MY SOLDIERS ARE RUNNING FROM THE BATTLE-FIELD. NO....NO....DON'T RUN!

SHATTERED IN MIND AND BODY, DURYODHANA, WITH MACE IN HAND, JUMPED INTO A POOL.

MY BODY BURNS WITH SHAME AND ANGER! THESE WATERS WILL COOL ME.

HIDING IN A POOL? DO YOU REPENT YOUR WICKED DEEDS AT LEAST NOW, DURYODHANA?

DURYODHANA WAS HURT.

I DON'T! ARE YOU WILLING TO FIGHT A DUEL?

COME OUT FIRST.

BHEEMA LEAPED LIKE A LION.

YOUR END TOO IS NEAR, DURYODHANA. TAKE IT ON THE THIGHS.

MORTALLY WOUNDED, DURYODHANA FELL TO THE GROUND.

YOUR INSULT TO DRAUPADI IS AVENGED.

THAT NIGHT ASHWATTHAMA, SON OF DRONA, SAT BROODING.

MY FATHER WAS KILLED BY DECEIT. I SHALL KILL THE PANDAVAS ALSO THE SAME WAY.

STEALTHILY HE APPROACHED THE PANDAVA CAMP WITH TWO FRIENDS. HE MISTOOK THE SONS OF THE PANDAVAS FOR THE PANDAVAS.

SH! THEY ARE ASLEEP.

ENTERING THE TENTS THEY KILLED THE OCCUPANTS IN THEIR SLEEP AND THEN SET FIRE TO THE CAMP.

DURYODHANA HEARD THE NEWS LYING WOUNDED ON THE BATTLE-FIELD.

GOOD! I CAN DIE HAPPILY NOW, ASHWATTHAMA.

THERE WAS GREAT SORROW IN THE PANDAVA CAMP. ALL THE SONS OF DRAUPADI HAD BEEN KILLED.

WE HAVE GAINED THE KINGDOM, BUT AT WHAT COST?

LORD KRISHNA CONSOLED THEM.

YUDHISHTHIRA! GRIEVE NOT OVER THE PAST. GO BACK TO HASTINAPURA AND RULE WISELY.

YUDHISHTHIRA RETURNED TO HASTINAPURA AND RULED IT FOR MANY MANY YEARS.